Festivals

Mardi Gras

by Rebecca Pettiford

Bullfrog Books

Ideas for Parents and Teacher

Bullfrog Books let children practice reading informational text at the earliest reading levels. Repetition, familiar words, and photo labels support early readers.

Before Reading
- Discuss the cover photo. What does it tell them?
- Look at the picture glossary together. Read and discuss the words.

Read the Book
- "Walk" through the book and look at the photos. Let the child ask questions. Point out the photo labels.
- Read the book to the child, or have him or her read independently.

After Reading
- Prompt the child to think more. Ask: Have you ever celebrated Mardi Gras? What sorts of things do you see during this festival?

Bullfrog Books are published by Jump!
5357 Penn Avenue South
Minneapolis, MN 55419
www.jumplibrary.com

Library of Congress Cataloging-in-Publication Data

Names: Pettiford, Rebecca, author.
Title: Mardi Gras / by Rebecca Pettiford.
Description: Minneapolis, MN: Jump!, Inc., [2017]
Series: Festivals | Includes index.
Identifiers: LCCN 2016026924 (print)
LCCN 2016028422 (ebook)
ISBN 9781620315347 (hard cover: alk. paper)
ISBN 9781620315880 (pbk.)
ISBN 9781624964886 (e-book)
Subjects: LCSH: Carnival—Louisiana—New Orleans—Juvenile literature. | New Orleans (La.)—Social life and customs—Juvenile literature.
Classification: LCC GT4211.N4 P47 2017 (print)
LCC GT4211.N4 (ebook) | DDC 394.2509763/35—dc23
LC record available at https://lccn.loc.gov/2016026924

Editor: Kirsten Chang
Book Designer: Leah Sanders
Photo Researcher: Leah Sanders

Photo Credits: All photos by Shutterstock except: Alamy, 8, 9, 14–15, 16–17, 23tl; AP Images, 16; Getty, 5, 18–19, 23br; iStock, 6–7, 24; JBKC/Shutterstock.com, 20–21.

Printed in the United States of America at Corporate Graphics in North Mankato, Minnesota.

Table of Contents

Fat Tuesday

It is the Tuesday before Lent.

It's time for Mardi Gras!

Mardi Gras means "Fat Tuesday" in French.

What is Lent?

A time to give up some pleasures.

But Mardi Gras is a time to have fun.

In New Orleans, we have a big party.

New Orleans

We dress up.

Bri wears a mask.

king cake

We eat king cake. Yum!

It is purple, green, and gold.

They are the colors of Mardi Gras.

A toy baby is hidden in the cake.

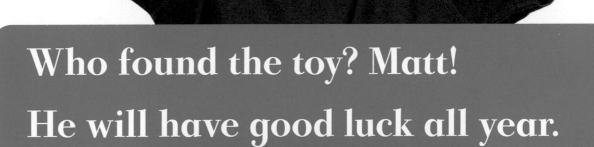

Who found the toy? Matt!

He will have good luck all year.

We go to
the parade.

Wow! Look
at the floats!

We yell, "Throw me something, Mister!"

People throw beads.

They throw coins.

Rex

18

Look! It's Rex!

He is King of Mardi Gras.

We play music.

We dance.

Mardi Gras is fun!

Symbols of Mardi Gras

mask

coins

beads

king cake

Picture Glossary

floats
Decorated stages built on trucks that move in a parade.

New Orleans
A city in Louisiana, a state in the southern United States.

Lent
A time when Christians repent for sin by giving up something, like meat or sugar.

parade
An outdoor march that celebrates a special day or event.

Index

To Learn More

Learning more is as easy as 1, 2, 3.

1) Go to www.factsurfer.com

2) Enter "MardiGras" into the search box.

3) Click the "Surf" button to see a list of websites.

With factsurfer.com, finding more information is just a click away.